RED LILY

RED LILY

POEMS

ISABEL ZUBER

Press 53
Winston-Salem, NC

Press 53
PO Box 30314
Winston-Salem, NC 27130

First Edition

Copyright © 2010 by Isabel Zuber

All rights reserved, including the right of reproduction in whole or in part in any form. For permission, contact author at Editor@Press53.com, or at the address above.

Cover design by Kevin Morgan Watson

Cover art, "Red Lily," copyright © 2010 Margaret Armfield

Isabel Zuber portrait by Anne Mercer Kessler Shields

Printed on acid-free paper

ISBN 978-1-935708-03-2

To Kay

Contents

AKNOWLEDGMENTS   ix

THE MARSH AT THE EDGE OF A DREAM   xi

THENS

OPEN, OPEN	3
HE SANG TO ME	4
YOUR OLD WAYS	5
WASP NEST	6
EARLY MARCH	7
TO SHARE	8
FOR HER	9
CEDAR SPRING	10
UNOBLIGED	11
GUIDED, A PATH	12
THE RULE FOR BEARING	14
AFTERMATH	15
WORKS OF ART	16
SOLSTICE	17
AND NOW, PILGRIM	18

NOWS

THE RUSH ON THROUGH	21
JUMP, JACK	23
EDEN	25
NIGHTWARD	26
SUDDENLY RAINING IN NOVEMBER	27

MISSING THE MILKY WAY	28
A MOON NAMED PINK	29
JULY	30
THE SHELL SAVER	31
COMMUNION	32
COME TO SEE ME	33
THAW	34
MIDWINTER	35
THE DECREASE OF THE TRIBE	36
FROM THE GARLIC PATCH	37
FAMILY GROUND	38
END OF OCTOBER	40
LISTEN, THE RIVER	41

NEVERS

KNELL	45
FAIR ENOUGH	46
THE BRIDE OF EARTH	47
CRAFT	48
AWASH WITH LOOSENED PETALS	49
CASTLE WALLS	50
MARGINALIA	52
SHE HAD SEEN	53
CATHERINE	54
SURCEASE	55
WHEN THE QUEEN	56
BANE AND SIMPLES	57
CRONING	58
THE RETURN	59
MALADY	60
THEY	61
THE FINE AND WAYWARD HORSES	62

Acknowledgments

Some of these poems have appeared in the following anthologies, chapbooks, and magazines.

The American Voice: "Marginalia"
The Arts Journal: "Craft," "The Marsh at the Edge of a Dream," "Open, Open"
Frontage Road: "Wasp Nest," "Cedar Spring"
The Georgia Journal: "July," "To Share," "Nightward"
The Greensboro Review: "Knell"
Images: "Come to see me"
Iris: "Jump, Jack"
Jackpine Press : "Solstice"
The Laurel Review: "The Shell Saver"
Mountain Home Companion: "Catherine," "Castle Walls," "The Fine and Wayward Horses"
Pembroke Magazine: "End of October," "Family Ground," "The Rush on Through"
Poetry: "Croning," "Missing the Milky Way," "Bane and Simples"
Primavera: "Surcease"
The Small Farm: "Thaw"
Whetstone: "The Decrease of the Tribe"

The Gritloaf Anthology: "Unobliged"
Old Wounds, New Words: "From the Garlic Patch"
Women of the Piedmont Triad: "Awash with Loosened Petals," "Malady," "The Return," "They"
Oriflamb: "Advent," "Fair Enough," "Your Old Ways"
Winter's Exile: "And Now, Pilgrim," "Early March," "He Sang to Me," "For Her," "Guided, A Path," "The Rule for Bearing," "Aftermath," "Works of Art"

The Marsh at the Edge of a Dream

I don't spend the days indoors,
not with these bare smoked walls,
little windows, thick, uncurtained,
and I here alone.

Outside, folds of weavable grass
whisper I need make nothing
useful of them. The water
murmurs I waste no time in choosing

a certain wet stone. I'm sure
of it. Tomorrow I will bake bread,
fry a few fish in case of company.
No one ever comes today.

Sing, sister little red lily.
Something will get carried on.

THENS

Open, Open

I want to put the album
in your lap, ask who is
this child with ribbons
in the back row? Do you
remember the woman
on the rock? Who is that
dark-haired man, kneeling,
arms around two little girls,
one wearing his big straw hat?
The people in your wedding party?
Whose funeral these flowers?
Who did up the braids
that caused such a look
of eternal surprise? Or
hung the swing for a young man
to lounge in, one hand
on his elegant narrow boot?
Where does that flight
of stone steps go? Out of the picture
to what trees, what house,
what lifelong love?

He Sang to Me

He sang to me
a long while back,
of harps hanging

on willow trees, of those
summer dying roses,
had winter's exile

in his voice even then
and I so young knew
the song sad but

didn't know why,
as sad then as now
when I do know.

Your Old Ways

How would I know
if your old ways
work? Is there more
promise, less risk, the right
amount of danger?

What are you waiting
to tell me? I raise
beds in the garden, graft
a bud, root my cuttings uneasily.

What is it I don't know
that might save us all?

Wasp Nest

If you wait till dark
you can take a pole
with rags doused
in kerosene,
burn the thing right up.
The trick is not
to catch the eaves. It
looks ash already,
that paper home, but
flames will light up
the wall and falling bodies.
Some get away but most
drop crisp or smoke-stunned.
Smash those underfoot,
in case. They're done
to death for nothing
except wanting some
of the cider,
coming for it armed.

Early March

"Cold
got the fig twigs
again this year—
I can tell.
Nothing
sharpens sense
of quick and dead
like a
long winter."

To Share

There was always enough.
The great old trees
were climbed and
black sweet fruit
rained by bucketfuls
filling our washtub,
staining like
too-rich blood.

Leaning on the fence
from time to time,
hand with a hot juice wound
shading my eyes, I watched
the long afternoon
in summer sun as he
at a distance in the next field
moved a slow shuttle's throw

bending to row by row.
From the marsh
redwings rose, gnats
wreathed the air
in the dusty roadway, and I
believed both the worker
and the task eternal.

For Her

    he cut locust poles
        in the woods,
        peeled, notched,
        joined and set them
        as an arbor,

planted a vine
    of pink grapes
    that she loved,

helped with the windows,
    she on the inside,
    he out, wiping spots,

smiled at her
    through shining glass,

brought her whatever
    he found strange or
    lovely—the first
    dandelion, a snail
    shell, whispering
    grasses' ears, bird's
    specked egg, a clear
    fine-shaped stone,

fixed breakfast,
    stayed near seventy years.

Cedar Spring

Because he remembered water
we went to find it, took him
back to seek that special place
of college outings, picnics,
apple-green courting days,
where a great free spring
gushed straight from the rock,
cold, pure, and broad
as the road it flowed across.
Red-winged blackbirds flocked there,
he said, and marsh grasses
he's seen growing nowhere else
stood tall beside the stream.

It would be there, he said,
for all time. What ever could
change a spring that big?
Because he was old we tried
and tried, drove the state park
by that name, came to parking lots,
the visitors' center, several streams,
but not their source. I see,
he said, I was wrong.
So springs go too.

Unobliged

"Don't
let the angel
bless you
before you
release him.
That's too much
responsibility.
You've got to go
found a nation
or something.
Keep it indefinite.
Most everything's best
unblessed."

Guided, A Path

My fields, he said, my land
and increase for my kind,
flung his arms over rows and rows
of autumn gathering
under a sharp, clear sky,

but the downward beckoned.
When someone waved in silence
from the edge of the woods
he went to see, following
the bare curved track

through yellowed stubble
into forest, into soundless dark
and then, seduced, he never stopped,
not even when leaves,
trees, branches, light

all vanished and
she came in gold
bearing a cradle
under a silken weaving
of webbed and circling flowers.

Lifting a corner, the golden beast
showed him the infant curled
inside, small, glowing, no
shape he could name
and yet he knew

contained therein
was all he had ever been
and all that he would be again
and that everything
every thing is kin.

THE RULE FOR BEARING

She reaches up
and with her finger
places a cross
on the window glass,
a mark
out of the heart's
own pain
but nothing
you could tell
anyone.

Aftermath

"I could have washed
and bleached everything,
put by what was needed,
put away what was not
but I can hardly bear
the way late sunlight
comes across the floor."

Works of Art

After the service
a friend speaks
to the widow. "You must
come to our class now.
We do still lifes,
have so much fun."

"I haven't even sketched
for years." But she takes in
particulars, Wednesday
mornings, the time, others
who will be there,
thinking the while
of a hot day, of him painting
the barn a deep dark red,
high on the ladder above her.

Solstice

Longest night
the sacred sweep
from light to dark,
dark to light.
We draw the rhythm
of our breath
rise, fall, ease, flow.

In the kitchen
a woman sings
hymns of another
time, an earlier
faith, and a winter
rose blooms on
the window sill.

And Now, Pilgrim

He has risen early to be on his way,
with his cap pushed back,
sleeves rolled up,
already a strong stride
on the long path home.
He is smiling into
the morning that now
will last him forever.

NOWS

The Rush on Through

I was born to my mother's dismay
with a lopsided face and a folded ear.
In time they would both straighten
but meanwhile she hid me from
visitors for her shame. She taped
my ear to my head, could not
nurse me, later told me she'd never seen
anything so ugly and that the color brown
had given her morning sickness.

I was born to my father's joy,
a fruitful end to five year's barrenness.
Miss Mary helped the doctor and
a cousin from the country
slipped an open pair of scissors
under the bed while skies rained down.
In the next room my father
waited all night, by morning
wrote in his journal, I hear a baby crying.

I had arrived suddenly
in the midst of a thunderstorm
and learned to walk in rain.
I flew through my childhood
on a wind so sharp & strong
it blew the lid off my lunchbox,
took the caps of postmen,
whistled in the chimneys,
turned doorknobs to get in.

From there to here
I have been brought
on moon-driven gales that
have since receded and now
await the hurricane.

Jump, Jack

Dumb doll, my sweet-
smiling idiot with indiscreet
charm, he'd leap for anyone
who pulled his leg, the elastic
thread on the top of his shiny

green head. From simple joy
his sinews gave out, spool
limbs no longer snapping back
against the wooden body
with its big buttons,

so my young uncles took him
to the dirt pile left where
the trench was dug for
rhubarb and blew him to
splinters with the rifle.

But first they taught me
how to shoot. My crazy
uncle half-knelt,
holding me like a small
tree to be climbed,

supporting the gun longer
than I was tall and my other
uncle said close one eye,
make that at the end of the barrel
show at the bottom of this here,

pull the trigger easy, gentle,
like stroking your cat. I've tried
somehow to hold it against them
but never could, after years
never wanted to paint

their old bald heads green,
get them in my sights
for we share deep mastery I mean
not to use but have, in any case.
Cheek against satin smooth stock

that fits my shoulder now
I can focus to a single vision,
draw a bead on a small loose-
jointed shape against fresh brown
earth. I can fire a bullet

like a caress. Old slow secret
stony knowledge carried
undelivered for some time, my uncles
and I, we know this, how to
make those clowns dance.

EDEN

In the photograph she is seated
on a folding chair at the edge
of the croquet lawn, poised, in white,
coolly elegant, holding an apple.

I have already been born.
My sister will soon be conceived.
Between the two of us,
her only children, she is
boyishly slim, seems untouched.

Off camera my father
and his brothers vie
under trees of uncertain knowledge
for whatever advantage mallets,
wickets, wooden balls, her attention,
can confer. She is smiling.

One cannot tell whether she has
bitten the apple or not, or if
she might ever have thought
to cast herself out instead
of staying all those years as she did.
No pictures were ever taken
that show her pregnant.

Nightward

A last enormous freedom
is to run into the dark,
barely enough day left
to see vague hydrangeas
massed along the drive
and junipers like spears
against the sky. Bound then

in the dusk with all that
can be there light says is not.
Rush the yard on grass-lashed,
bug-bit legs, turn round
and round till stars collide
with spires, breaking the
huge dinning noise
of all those tiny voices.

Such venture is less, or more,
than brave, for dew's sweet
or bitter, and there's always
the lighted doorway and
the sense that if one runs
far and hard enough
there are arms in the darkness also.

Suddenly Raining in November

When it went dark
by noon ditches
filled immediately.
Two chicken flocks
and a convertible
were washed away.
Grandmother,
Old Grandmother, I fear
these times are abusive
and not well controlled.
Measures taken
on the site of the previous
flood availed nothing.

Far to the mountains
strange weather is forming-
clouds like stone,
a full and heavy wind
that will reach us
by tonight. I read
a map in the folds
of a dishtowel, those arrows
of direction, can interpret
steam warnings from
the kettle and think
this house may stand.

There was no one
in the convertible. I thought
you would want to know.

Missing the Milky Way

It's late and no moon,
no bright disk with
the gaunt rabbit crouching
on its surface. I walk
my yard till Arcturus
lodges at the top of a pine,

bear guardian scaled down
to ornament. His kind are
faint and few, for my neighbors
favor big bright lights,
loud music to keep
themselves safe. The cost

to me of their security
is any quiet night, frogs
calling, "Hello, over here,
over here," any number of
stars distant and various
and most unnamed.

A Moon Named Pink

After mowing till sundown
I wait for a moon named pink
who rises a wonder, more gold
than rose, over my neighbor's trees
while I watch till she clears
the top new leafing branch.

Next month she comes
as flower moon, and each fullness
thereafter rounds to a different name.
Old stilled tongues her changes called
for heat and snow, corn, sap, worms
hunters and fog, harvest,

bucks, cold and wolves.
By her they timed and tamed
a riot of life, their toil,
meaning in her measure given to
planting, birth, journeys, hunts.
With a glass left for me after work

I toast departed namers,
those long-gone observers,
then finally drink the moon herself,
aglow in reflecting water, to call down
on us all shadow-borne power of same,
yet ever changing, mystery.

July

Purple basil tries
the cracks of the sidewalk,
tomatoes riot
in the front yard
and a bag of cement
has been left on the porch.
I pass, afraid to linger,
looking in, taking on

these days long walks
in the heat scented
with spoilage, faint with
thunder far off. Even
ivy wants to wilt
and the pulse insists
forget, forget.

At a time like this
once meant for memory,
how much could be caught
in waves rising on the street,
a fan moving a curtain,
someone turning
away from the bed.

The Shell Saver

How dare they my children
dash to the water
as if it wouldn't
drown them quickly
if it could.
The waves take them well
beyond my reach. They
think my fears are funny.

I select shells on the shore
in the shallows at the edge.
I take only the thin,
thinner than glass—palest,
most fragile—ones the
ocean would smash to pieces
with the next wave
if it could.

Communion

Midnight
and the smell wakens them.
My children stagger
out of sleep and into my kitchen,
lured by fragrance, two loaves
fresh from the oven. Would they,
I wonder, rouse as well if
our house were burning down,
which, in a sense, it is.

Certainly something consumes
the life we had, means that now
dough must be kneaded at dusk,
set to rise after dark. But in this hour
by lamplight we bring out my mother's
long black bread knife, honey, raspberry
jam, eat one whole loaf together,
fear held off with bread, hot milk.
We leave the crumbs for mice
and tomorrow.

Come to See Me

Accept this house.
It smells of onions,
wet shoes, hair unwashed.
The wasps fly in
all summer, can't find
what they want to eat
and die on the floor.

You've not been here
for so long you'll
find me changed.
I wear a shawl in
the evenings, curse
God and sometimes
beat my fist on the wall.

Thaw

The wind
Went tender
Of a sudden
Lost
January leanness

We sat
On the porch
A mild winter
I said
False spring
She said

The difference
Sat between us

Midwinter

Lord, love,
how I would like
to be surprised,
relieved,
to know by
tiny tokens
afloat in midwinter's
changing light,
—those proofs,
mites and midges—
that we've not
killed everything.

THE DECREASE OF THE TRIBE

They have sold an L of acreage for
a new plant that makes a part
of something that is a part of
something that controls emissions.
Boards are falling off the barn.
Burdock grows in the lane.
No garden planted this year.

She elevates her feet on
a stool as she quilts. He spits
tobacco juice into a paper cup
and reads his books, the paper.
The table is spread with
a white cloth, some wildflowers,
and it is very quiet.

From the hill where peacocks
scream for the peahens stolen
last fall you can see the new
highway in the valley, always
with trucks. The fat pony
grazing has not been
bridled for years.

Since I was here they've
sold all the pigs, are down
to the cow. The gamebirds
fight and kill each other off.
One wet and dead I came across
under the boxwood. You will
find us much changed, she said.

From the Garlic Patch

If it rains long enough
the leak will drill through
roof and ceiling,
spread a puddle
on the floor. I used
to worry about such things.
Now someone else can battle rust,
mold, whatever creeps up to the door.
I haven't sewn on a button
in ages and smoke from the fire
gives me a cough. Let bygones
be drybones. I'll stew
what I've got, eat it when I want to.
Why don't you go wear down
your broom on your own porch?
One of these nights
I'll ride naked over all of you.

Family Ground

At time's end
God is to sound for them,
all these lying close, left here
on this high ridge, visited
by wind so rough
it's taken half of every tree.

Their feet
are mostly to the east, except
for one or two who'll
have to rise up sideways.
The wind's their only everlasting
guest, always coming,

leaving,
whistling through the bed
spring gate, tangling
wreaths and ribbons in the fence.
Under the peach, two lilacs,
a pot of old-hen-little-chickens,

mounds of
white gravel, Wanda
and Earl are together again,
Robert, Viola, Emma too, and
several others who've
already lost their names.

Good earth
is kept for the living. This
rocky soil's so thin and shallow
that perhaps—Hallo!—one day
a next-to-last trump! The wind
in a generous companionable mood

arriving before God,
throwing back the covers.
Get up. High time. Come away!
So off they'll all go, particle
by particle, out over the valley,
into distance, on to the far and shining sea.

End of October

Tonight's their time but they came early,
have been here all day, watching
from among the trees, rustling faded grass.
They speak in whispers too low for sound,
seem to approve the way we've let the place
go to wild and ruin, its hedges pokeweed—
bright, beautiful poison—
tangles of rose, honeysuckle.

Clouds come and go as I hang out the clothes
while they still observe it all. Then later
I sense what could have been their breath
as I unpin warmed white sheets,
sun-fragrant towels, the shirts.

Do they think they've been summoned?
I know better, yet
strain to hear voices in the leaves.
"Why have you left me?" they call.
I could ask them "Who left whom? Which
are you?" but to the evening's strange
and rising wind I say nothing. They linger
for any who will listen but by now
they have no differences
and all their smiles are grave.

Listen, the River

Listen, the river is longing
to drown you. Hear how
the wind lusts to blow
you away. But earth
says bed down, now bed down.
You are mine, you are mine,
you are mine.

NEVERS

KNELL

Remember the fish
that swallowed the church,
how the minister for once
fell full silent, and then
the whole thing was spat out
on the bottom of the sea,
steeple still intact, bell swinging,
clapper free. For a long time
bubbles rose from the organ pipes,
and members of the choir—
robes spreading slowly, dark,
gently as if they belonged there—
floated up against the windows,
their faces pressed to clear places
in the glass, mouths round
as if saying oh, look!
there are no sights like these in air.

Fair Enough

A tangle loosened, the cord
pulls taut again. As if listening
my head turns so that I look out
the door down the hall through
archways into the garden. My chair's
fixed at an angle so I cannot miss
the statues of martyrs. They've
been gotten up as nymphs and naiades,
experiencing what was never intended.

When I am allowed to rise, the floor
of inlay appears aslant. A promising
window becomes plaster wall, its vision
flat paint. For this sullen time I wear
silk flowers, eat some of those cakes
of tasteless paste. They make one ache.

There was once something
here in the fountain whose word
I forget but it is said a toy frog
fell into the works. If you tell me
there are other ways, I may not believe
you. Indeed, I cannot believe you.

THE BRIDE OF EARTH

The bride of earth
has eaten the fruit
of knowledge and love.

Out of sun and favor
she grows pale, a pallor
scarcely noticed for

her lover's skin
is paler, his hair
cold black. Deep

underground they
play at draughts with
diamonds and coal,

and when she sings
to him the columns
of crystal salt ring.

For love, for a season,
she has forgotten her mother
and what others need to live.

CRAFT

Move the thread
she did tied a
thousand thousand
knots chains flowers
What do you
make I said
A snare Oh I
thought it was lace
She held it to her face
What do you think
lace is anyway

Awash With Loosened Petals

In this place with all suspended, no bowl
will hold water, no flame stand. You had
thought to make a presentation of your tears
but, as I say, nothing can be held.
Your tears hang in the air, a distance
away from you. A candle burns sideways
and no footfall is heard. Be you
generous, gentle and unrestrained and
you will fare well here. Farewell here.

Castle Walls

Below this window
the river flows, slow,
waterweeded, dark. Thick
tangles choke the bank and a tree
has fallen yonder side.
Small bones whiten
on sandbars. I never
pull the curtain back.

My other window
opens to the south garden—
mignonette, pinks, nicotiana,
a great many butterflies.
I shall sit there, dip
my pen, move smooth words
across vellum, study not to
be afraid. Yesterday in a

pitch-daubed basket, a babe
went by on the water. I
did not look out though I've
been childless nine long years.
Tomorrow a stone boat will come
oared by men with visors down.
They have no faces now. Stone
will scrape on stone and

a queen will come to land.
In darkness tonight—all
halls and rooms still under
trembling ivy, with rats
skittering behind the panels—
everyone in this castle
will lie silent but awake,
waiting for our queen.

Marginalia

The edges of another's work
were all the space
she had for her story.
With grease and lamp black,
a fine point, she set down
her worth in small letters
that she might abide.
Ruffle the pages of an old book.
Perhaps you will glimpse her.

She Had Seen

She had seen
the oats and wheat
plaited separately,
plaited together,
and guessed
at what they meant
since no one knew.

Study, she said.
More, she said, when
they asked what
she wanted. To know
more. Too much lost.

But then
her hand
was around his neck.
His hand was on her
waist. Her head was
on his shoulder, her
breasts against
his chest, his face
against her hair,
his thigh between
her legs. Knowledge.

Catherine

This fine house turns its back
on the north field. Wind comes down
dying, not often, by evening.
Leave your couch. Open the window.
Bring in suffering, bring in cold.
I get weak in your rose-round
warmth with nothing to push
against, all this yielding.
The arm I need for fighting
will be too wasted to wield
a needle. Be warned, I have
a weapon left, a hook so tiny you
can hardly see it. While you aren't
looking I slip it into your glass.
Later, as you sleep, by thread invisible
I wind out of you what I want
most from inside—that key of mine
you swallowed to keep me here.
Open the stupid window. You've
left so little air a lapwing
would suffocate. If you don't open
the window I shall run out by the
low door, barefoot, dancing
the hard ice-crusted snow
under endless and blackened stars.

Surcease

Ride round by the low tower,
through thick wet grass, over
last year's leaves pliant as leather.
Brush aside the webs heavy
with rain to enter.
Be welcome. This is our place,
for the weaving here is excellent.
There are seats by the fire
and a child who must never be struck
will bring something to drink.

We shall have a song after supper
in a forbidden mode,
perhaps some talk of life
in a damp climate.
Rest unconcerned.
No former wives are to be
found in any unused room,
neatly laid out in rows,
wearing their best.

When the Queen

When the queen hurried to
the garden to plead for
her life her judges were

nearly assembled, a
cold stone whetting an edge.
Heads of tall gaudy gay

dahlias nodded beside
the thyme-scented path. By
stifling then a private

theology she put
hand to her embroidered
heart, swore eternal faith,

and spoke so fair she saved
herself while her soul shrank
to the size of a fine

silver thimble. Something,
she thought, almost that small
could hold all of her blood.

BANE AND SIMPLES

A current physic
curses me, administered
without trial, insight,

for recovery or else.
I war among prescriptions,
tear off labels, jumble

pills. It doesn't matter.
Some remedy or other
will seek me. I can't hide.

Old practitioner,
wherever you believe,
is cure there? In plant,

dull bone, grass,
hank of hair, a touch,
the outlawed prayer?

CRONING

We were once women,
mourned the months
we did or did not conceive,

wept, clapped at your
every departure. We
starved for the whim

of fashion, grew fat
for pleasure, lay in beds
that bent and crackled

while stars on trial
for eternity suddenly
changed their positions.

Thunder shook down
our houses, deception
built them up again.

In spite of ourselves
we came at last
to the evil of being

extremely learned,
none of our knowledge
a comfort.

The Return

"If I thought not to hear again
my steps in the high vaulted hall,
if I did not dream torches doubled,
redoubled, fire in the many mirrors,
if I did not see in mind that
whole grave company coming nobly
down the bannered stairs to greet us,
how could I, we, go on? It has been
years and surely more miles than round
the earth, all for the time that we
feast once more at the long table, wear
fresh clothing without the stains of battle,
and hear the songs of our own deeds."

So they did not tell him the scouts had said
only ruins beyond on the ashen plain,
quiet and cold in autumn rain.

Malady

When shall I take
an ancient trace, bolting
from brush and bracken
a soul new-sinewed and
no longer human? Or
mount the storm, carried
in currents and channels
where I'd drown but for
my wings? When crawl
sand of deepest waters,
ungrowing my eyes in
the dark? It has been

believed that from this
storied fabled tower
perimeters of the universe
could be glimpsed, so
it did not seem to matter
there was no way out,
no way in, or that on
the flood plain below
daily waters rise, recede,
casting up mysteries,
washing them away again.

They

After we had destroyed them all
we came to worship their art,
would sit for hours in conquered, fretted
doorways to watch the play of fountains
on paved courtyards, fondling the while
those carved stone dogs. We wrapped ourselves
in sinuous robes of a fabric we could
not name, hid our rough invaders' faces
behind bland masks with narrow plucked brows.
The smoke of pipes polished as water
curled from our nostrils. We drank
the bitterest, the most severe of all
their remedies, forgot our own memories.
Flute, drums moved our bodies in dances
we never made and in time we prayed
to the very gods who could not save them.

The Fine and Wayward Horses

We ride
the fine and wayward
horses of the night
not knowing
how we got on their backs
ride without reins.
They have never known breaking
plunge every cliff
gallop the bottom of the sea.

Deceit, says a voice
under the wild wind.
You've been nowhere.

Hush we know more now
than saltwater or falling forever
and we go anywhere.

ISABEL ZUBER was born and grew up in Boone, North Carolina, when it was a small town with few traffic problems. She graduated from Appalachian State University and received a master's degree from the University of North Carolina at Greensboro. She has been a librarian, a small press publisher, a gardener, an inventive vegetarian cook, and a homemaker. She has served on the boards of the North Carolina Writers Network, the Salem Center for Women Writers, and the Grassy Creek Neighborhood Alliance.

Her poetry and short fiction have appeared in *Poetry*, *The American Voice*, *The Small Farm*, *The Greensboro Review*, *The Arts Journal*, *Now and Then*, *Pembroke Magazine*, *The Laurel Review*, *The Southern Review*, *Shenandoah*, *Sandhills Review*, *Cave Wall*, and other magazines.

She has published two collections of poetry, *Oriflamb*, which won the North Carolina Writers Network chapbook prize, and *Winter's Exile*, poems for her father. Her novel *Salt* was published by Picador in 2002 and was given the First Novel Award from Virginia Commonwealth University that year.

She has received a Forsyth County Arts Council grant and, in 2009, a North Carolina Arts Council fellowship.

Isabel lives in Winston-Salem, North Carolina, and is the mother of a grown son and daughter.

Cover artist **MARGARET (PRISSY) ARMFIELD** lives in Clemmons, North Carolina. She has a studio at home and in the arts district of Winston-Salem. She is a sculptor of portrait busts and relief sculpture in clay and bronze. She is an artist also in oil and pastels. Her love of nature is expressed in her paintings. She has studied many years with other artists in both fields.

A deep appreciation for all those who taught, influenced and supported along the way. This collection is dedicated to Kay Byer, who has been the best friend anyone could ever ask for. It is coming into being through the interest of Kevin Watson of Press 53. And there are many others whose help and friendship have made an invaluable difference. Among them are Fred Chappell, Archie Ammons, Lee Smith, Ed and Emily Wilson, Charles and Ruth Price, Heather Ross Miller, Becky Gibson, Clarke and Peggy Garrett, Elizabeth Phillips, Graydon Eggers, Tommy Thompson, David Hodgin, Cratis Williams, Darnell Arnoult, Michael McFee. Anne and David Bailey, Sarah Lindsay, Anne Barnhill, Ellen Daughman, Marita Garin, Leigh McMillan, Beverly Johnston, Tony Abbott, and all the members of reading and writing groups and workshops who have shared with me through the years. A special love to my family, my son Jon, my daughter Liz, my son-in-law Chris, and my sister Beth, who is also a poet. And with happy memories of my parents, Herman and Elizabeth Eggers, who gave me the precious gift of love for the written and the spoken word.

I.Z.

www.ingramcontent.com/pod-product-compliance
Lightning Source LLC
Chambersburg PA
CBHW051712040426
42446CB00008B/847